fluent*ish*

Language: _____

Property of: _____

Started: ___ /___ /___

Completed: ___ /___ /___

Teach®
Yourself

fluent*ish*

Language Learning
Planner and Journal

Set goals, track habits,
organize notes, and tell your
story in a new language

Jo Franco

First published by Teach Yourself in 2023
An imprint of John Murray Press

1

Copyright © Jo Franco

A CIP catalogue record for this title is available from the British Library

Hardback ISBN 9781399805926
ebook ISBN 9781399805933

Text design by Nicky Barneby, Barneby *design & art direction*

Printed and bound in China

John Murray Press policy is to use papers that are natural, renewable
and recyclable products and made from wood grown in sustainable forests.
The logging and manufacturing processes are expected to conform to
the environmental regulations of the country of origin.

John Murray Press
Carmelite House
50 Victoria Embankment
London EC4Y 0DZ

Nicholas Brealey Publishing
Hachette Book Group
Market Place, Center 53, USA

www.teachyourself.com

John Murray Press, part of Hodder & Stoughton Limited
An Hachette UK company

Contents

What is fluent*ish*?

In the world of language learning there's one thing that *never gets lost in translation*: It's almost impossible to define the word "fluent."

Is it defined by acing an online quiz that blurts out "You're a level C2" on the CEFR (Common European Framework of Reference)? Or a test that labels you "Superior" on the ACTFL (American Council of Teaching Foreign Languages) scale? Does fluency count if you only *speak* the language? Or do you need to be a master wordsmith when it comes to *writing* in the language, too? What about the reality that one day you wake up feeling confident in the language, and a few weeks later you struggle to express yourself in the most basic ways—are you still fluent then? What if you can only speak with conviction while giving a monologue in a classroom setting, but choke with the stress of speaking in the real world? Let's be real: Are we even fluent in our native tongue to the degree where we can describe the intricacies of quantum physics, or explain our plumbing problems with sophistication?

The beauty is in the progress, not the perfection, especially when it comes to language learning. So, I have embraced being fluent*ish* instead. I see my obstacles as my opportunities and focus my energy on learning one page, and one mistake, at a time.

I've crafted this journal to help you become fluent*ish*, too . . . whatever that means for you.

Jo Franco

Introduction

"A goal without a plan is just a wish."
—Antoine de Saint-Exupéry

You have just invested in two very powerful language learning tools in one book: journaling and planning. These two things can, and often are, done separately. But combining them can transform your language journey toward being fluent*ish*.

Why journal in your new language?

Some of the most successful people have kept journals, from Leonardo da Vinci to Oprah Winfrey. Scientifically speaking, old-fashioned paper and pen have done wonders for the human mind and memory. Not only does journaling and writing things down carve space in your mind to retain new information, but it also creates a body and mind connection. Writing in a new language, even at the nascent stage, will help you better retain what you've studied and immediately start personalizing your learning journey by focusing on the language you need and that is most meaningful to you. In other words, journaling in your target language helps you create context through your own connections.

Whether you're learning your first new language, or your sixth, journaling will inspire you to be creative and playful in your studies and keep the journey fresh and inspiring. It'll remove the academic undertone of the learning process and make it more about self-expression. After all, don't we learn languages to actually use them? What's the point of studying Spanish if you can't answer a basic dinner party question like "What's your dream job?"?

Journaling in a new language is like hiding the vitamins in the brownie: You learn a language while embarking on the ever-fascinating quest for self-discovery. And that, my friends, is the definition of a win-win. By the end of this journey, you'll not only have learned more of your target language, but you'll also have discovered hidden treasures within yourself. At the end of this book, you will find journal prompts, organized by level, to inspire your thoughts and get you writing you story in your new language. If your need extra suggestions, visit **www.joclub. world/fluent** for more resources.

Learn how YOU learn and make a plan

"Jo, how do you learn languages?" asks everyone on the internet.

My response: *"Language learning isn't 'one size fits all.'"*

There's not one magical app, book, or audio program that will make you fluent. You need to use loads of different methods and materials to create a collection of tools and techniques that are engaging and interesting to *you*. But with the overwhelming amount of material today, how do you break through the clutter of content and create a logical and customized pathway to fluency? I've got you.

That's exactly what the planner section of this book is designed to help you do. It's a framework based on the best practices in language learning that gives you a simple system and set of learning tools to follow. It combines the power of goal setting and habit tracking to make sure you are clear about what you're trying to achieve, keeping you accountable by tracking the small steps you need to get there.

Any language learner knows it's important to make the process fun, and to use the language daily, so my goal for you is to look forward to opening this language journal. Every time you write in it, you will open more of your mind and increase your potential.

With your fluen*tish* journal, not only will you be investing in yourself by committing to maintaining these new habits, but you can also connect to a global community of journalers in **JoClub Fluent** who are all on a journey to grow their languages, too. Who knows, you might even meet your language buddy on the other side of the world!

About the author

Hi, I'm Jo, the person who leaves pen stains behind me wherever I go. It's a bad habit, but it's the price I pay for having to write everything down. But to be honest, writing didn't come easy—at least not in English.

Throughout this journal you'll write your own story in a new language, but first I figured I should tell you mine, and how I became fluent*ish* in six-plus languages: Portuguese, French, Spanish, English, Italian, Greek, and Egyptian Arabic. (You can also find out more about what I do on **www.joclub.world**, the journaling company I founded, and on Instagram @jo_franco, or you can watch me as one of the hosts of the Netflix series *The World's Most Amazing Vacation Rentals*).

Born in Rio de Janeiro, Brazil, I was four years old when I read my first book in Portuguese. My grandma, a retired teacher, would sit me on her lap in the *escolinha*, or little school house, that doubled as a shed filled with books from floor to ceiling. There we would sit on small stools for our daily reading sessions while my older siblings were at school. Day after day she taught me how to make the right sounds by looking at markings on the yellowed pages of books that she'd used for decades to teach her students. I loved the smell of the books, and how words on paper would transport us to bright faraway lands without ever leaving the dark shed. It was magic.

My grandmother was stern, and I craved her approval. Each time I read a sentence, I took note of her surprise. It motivated me to keep going. So, at four years old, I mastered writing all four of my very long Brazilian names.

Just when I started getting the hang of speaking, writing, and reading in Portuguese, my mom brought my two siblings and me to small-town USA where we left everything we knew behind: family, friends, and fluency. I was five years old.

As the foreign brown girl in the class with a head full of curly hair and nowhere to hide it, I buried myself in books for English learners. My accent couldn't be judged if I stayed quiet. By age seven I caught on to the concept of being fluent*ish*: If I didn't totally understand what was happening, I was passed off as dumb. However, if I understood enough English to then translate it into Portuguese and help other students, I was suddenly smart. A few years into this linguistic limbo, I became a language hero in the school, and helped the new foreign kids who came after me feel more at home.

From that moment on I saw language as a superpower. It allowed me to toggle between various identities, like a spy. Before hitting double digits in age, I was determined to learn as many languages as possible to connect with the world, and learn more about myself one language at a time.

Only there was a massive problem: I never really loved school. I felt awkward and misunderstood, and rarely followed the pack. Instead, I set out on a path to learn languages my own way. Six languages later (and counting!), I've refined my technique, tools, and recommendations and it's these I'll walk you through in this language learning journal.

You are not like everyone else, so your learning path shouldn't be like all the others out there either.

You can follow me for more tips and inspiration on:

 @jo_franco

 @jofranco

www.jofranco.world

www.joclub.world/fluent

 @joclub_

My fluent*ish* journey

In all great transformations, it's critical to document where you start—even if you're starting in the middle. Where you are today will not be where you'll be tomorrow if you create a language learning lifestyle.

Remember, you want to learn this language and investing in this journal, journey, and practice is an act of self-compassion. This process isn't easy, so it's important to remember your why. Here are some questions to help you.

Why am I learning this language? How will it change my life? (Think: physically, emotionally, financially, spiritually.)

....
....
....
....
....
....
....
....
....
....
....
....

Describe what you want to be able to do in your new language?

....
....
....
....
....
....
....

Describe what your life will look like once you improve your language skills.

....
....
....
....
....
....
....
....

Rate how you feel about your current skill levels from 1 to 7 in the following areas. Where do you want to focus your learning? You can revisit this periodically to evaluate your progress.

How will I keep myself accountable? (A study buddy? Pay for a course? Online tutoring?)

1. . . . .
2. . . . .
3. . . . .

How often will I commit to studying and for how long? (Weekly, monthly?)

. . . .
. . . .
. . . .

What will I tell myself when I hit a wall or begin to plateau?

. . . .
. . . .
. . . .
. . . .

What does fun language learning look like?

. . . .
. . . .
. . . .
. . . .

What good habits do I need to start?

. . . .
. . . .
. . . .

What bad habits do I need to let go of?

. . . .
. . . .
. . . .

My resources

The best part of learning a language is opening your world to content you'd never find otherwise.

Consider this your treasure map where you'll take note of all the gems you've found useful to better your language skills and your knowledge of the world, and sprinkle some fun on your roadmap to becoming fluent*ish*.

Movies/TV shows	How can this help me?

Blogs/Websites/Newletters	How can this help me?

Podcasts

How can this help me?

....
....
....
....
....
....
....
....
....

Books/Magazines/Newspapers

How can this help me?

....
....
....
....
....
....
....
....
....
....

Social media accounts

How can this help me?

....
....
....
....
....
....
....
....

Apps   How can this help me?

....
....
....
....
....
....
....
....
....
....
....

Online courses/Tutors   How can this help me?

....
....
....
....
....
....
....
....
....
....
....

YouTube channels/Videos   How can this help me?

....
....
....
....
....
....
....
....
....
....

Other

How can this help me?

Habit tracker

Since learning anything requires commitment and consistency, using a monthly habit tracker is essential to keep you on track as you build your new language and new life.

Think of this as holistic immersion: You're in charge of designing your multilingual life. Whether you want to sleep more, drink more water, exercise, study for two hours a day, or commit to daily lessons with a tutor, **use this section to stay accountable.** In my experience, finding ways to integrate the language in my daily routine is the most sustainable and entertaining way to tackle an otherwise overwhelming task. Do the things you already do, just translate them into your target language.

Make sure you start small and build up one or two good habits at a time before adding more. And, if possible, try to combine two activities like listening to an audio course while going for a walk, for efficiency's sake.

With journaling, page by page you write a book. And with this journal, day by day and habit by habit, you learn a language.

Sambil menyelam, minum air.

While diving, drink water.

or

Accomplish two things at once.

Indonesian idiom

Habit tracker

Month: _____

This month I want to focus on:

Put a ★ for habits you can stack together.

Key: Completed ● Partial ◑ Missed ○

Habit	1	2	3	4	5	6	7	8	9	10	11	12	13	14	15	16	17	18	19	20	21	22	23	24	25	26	27	28	29	30	31
	○	○	○	○	○	○	○	○	○	○	○	○	○	○	○	○	○	○	○	○	○	○	○	○	○	○	○	○	○	○	○
	○	○	○	○	○	○	○	○	○	○	○	○	○	○	○	○	○	○	○	○	○	○	○	○	○	○	○	○	○	○	○
	○	○	○	○	○	○	○	○	○	○	○	○	○	○	○	○	○	○	○	○	○	○	○	○	○	○	○	○	○	○	○
	○	○	○	○	○	○	○	○	○	○	○	○	○	○	○	○	○	○	○	○	○	○	○	○	○	○	○	○	○	○	○
	○	○	○	○	○	○	○	○	○	○	○	○	○	○	○	○	○	○	○	○	○	○	○	○	○	○	○	○	○	○	○
	○	○	○	○	○	○	○	○	○	○	○	○	○	○	○	○	○	○	○	○	○	○	○	○	○	○	○	○	○	○	○
	○	○	○	○	○	○	○	○	○	○	○	○	○	○	○	○	○	○	○	○	○	○	○	○	○	○	○	○	○	○	○
	○	○	○	○	○	○	○	○	○	○	○	○	○	○	○	○	○	○	○	○	○	○	○	○	○	○	○	○	○	○	○
	○	○	○	○	○	○	○	○	○	○	○	○	○	○	○	○	○	○	○	○	○	○	○	○	○	○	○	○	○	○	○
	○	○	○	○	○	○	○	○	○	○	○	○	○	○	○	○	○	○	○	○	○	○	○	○	○	○	○	○	○	○	○

Habit tracker

Month: _____

This month I want to focus on:

Put a ★ for habits you can stack together.

Key: Completed ● Partial ◑ Missed ○

Habit	1	2	3	4	5	6	7	8	9	10	11	12	13	14	15	16	17	18	19	20	21	22	23	24	25	26	27	28	29	30	31
	○	○	○	○	○	○	○	○	○	○	○	○	○	○	○	○	○	○	○	○	○	○	○	○	○	○	○	○	○	○	○
	○	○	○	○	○	○	○	○	○	○	○	○	○	○	○	○	○	○	○	○	○	○	○	○	○	○	○	○	○	○	○
	○	○	○	○	○	○	○	○	○	○	○	○	○	○	○	○	○	○	○	○	○	○	○	○	○	○	○	○	○	○	○
	○	○	○	○	○	○	○	○	○	○	○	○	○	○	○	○	○	○	○	○	○	○	○	○	○	○	○	○	○	○	○
	○	○	○	○	○	○	○	○	○	○	○	○	○	○	○	○	○	○	○	○	○	○	○	○	○	○	○	○	○	○	○
	○	○	○	○	○	○	○	○	○	○	○	○	○	○	○	○	○	○	○	○	○	○	○	○	○	○	○	○	○	○	○
	○	○	○	○	○	○	○	○	○	○	○	○	○	○	○	○	○	○	○	○	○	○	○	○	○	○	○	○	○	○	○
	○	○	○	○	○	○	○	○	○	○	○	○	○	○	○	○	○	○	○	○	○	○	○	○	○	○	○	○	○	○	○
	○	○	○	○	○	○	○	○	○	○	○	○	○	○	○	○	○	○	○	○	○	○	○	○	○	○	○	○	○	○	○
	○	○	○	○	○	○	○	○	○	○	○	○	○	○	○	○	○	○	○	○	○	○	○	○	○	○	○	○	○	○	○
	○	○	○	○	○	○	○	○	○	○	○	○	○	○	○	○	○	○	○	○	○	○	○	○	○	○	○	○	○	○	○

Habit tracker

Month: _____

This month I want to focus on:

Put a ★ for habits you can stack together.

Key: Completed ● Partial ◐ Missed ○

Habit	1	2	3	4	5	6	7	8	9	10	11	12	13	14	15	16	17	18	19	20	21	22	23	24	25	26	27	28	29	30	31
	○	○	○	○	○	○	○	○	○	○	○	○	○	○	○	○	○	○	○	○	○	○	○	○	○	○	○	○	○	○	○
	○	○	○	○	○	○	○	○	○	○	○	○	○	○	○	○	○	○	○	○	○	○	○	○	○	○	○	○	○	○	○
	○	○	○	○	○	○	○	○	○	○	○	○	○	○	○	○	○	○	○	○	○	○	○	○	○	○	○	○	○	○	○
	○	○	○	○	○	○	○	○	○	○	○	○	○	○	○	○	○	○	○	○	○	○	○	○	○	○	○	○	○	○	○
	○	○	○	○	○	○	○	○	○	○	○	○	○	○	○	○	○	○	○	○	○	○	○	○	○	○	○	○	○	○	○
	○	○	○	○	○	○	○	○	○	○	○	○	○	○	○	○	○	○	○	○	○	○	○	○	○	○	○	○	○	○	○
	○	○	○	○	○	○	○	○	○	○	○	○	○	○	○	○	○	○	○	○	○	○	○	○	○	○	○	○	○	○	○
	○	○	○	○	○	○	○	○	○	○	○	○	○	○	○	○	○	○	○	○	○	○	○	○	○	○	○	○	○	○	○
	○	○	○	○	○	○	○	○	○	○	○	○	○	○	○	○	○	○	○	○	○	○	○	○	○	○	○	○	○	○	○
	○	○	○	○	○	○	○	○	○	○	○	○	○	○	○	○	○	○	○	○	○	○	○	○	○	○	○	○	○	○	○
	○	○	○	○	○	○	○	○	○	○	○	○	○	○	○	○	○	○	○	○	○	○	○	○	○	○	○	○	○	○	○
	○	○	○	○	○	○	○	○	○	○	○	○	○	○	○	○	○	○	○	○	○	○	○	○	○	○	○	○	○	○	○

Habit tracker

Month: _____

This month I want to focus on:

Put a ★ for habits you can stack together.

Key: Completed ● Partial ◑ Missed ○

Habit	1	2	3	4	5	6	7	8	9	10	11	12	13	14	15	16	17	18	19	20	21	22	23	24	25	26	27	28	29	30	31
....	○	○	○	○	○	○	○	○	○	○	○	○	○	○	○	○	○	○	○	○	○	○	○	○	○	○	○	○	○	○	○
....	○	○	○	○	○	○	○	○	○	○	○	○	○	○	○	○	○	○	○	○	○	○	○	○	○	○	○	○	○	○	○
....	○	○	○	○	○	○	○	○	○	○	○	○	○	○	○	○	○	○	○	○	○	○	○	○	○	○	○	○	○	○	○
....	○	○	○	○	○	○	○	○	○	○	○	○	○	○	○	○	○	○	○	○	○	○	○	○	○	○	○	○	○	○	○
....	○	○	○	○	○	○	○	○	○	○	○	○	○	○	○	○	○	○	○	○	○	○	○	○	○	○	○	○	○	○	○
....	○	○	○	○	○	○	○	○	○	○	○	○	○	○	○	○	○	○	○	○	○	○	○	○	○	○	○	○	○	○	○
....	○	○	○	○	○	○	○	○	○	○	○	○	○	○	○	○	○	○	○	○	○	○	○	○	○	○	○	○	○	○	○
....	○	○	○	○	○	○	○	○	○	○	○	○	○	○	○	○	○	○	○	○	○	○	○	○	○	○	○	○	○	○	○
....	○	○	○	○	○	○	○	○	○	○	○	○	○	○	○	○	○	○	○	○	○	○	○	○	○	○	○	○	○	○	○
....	○	○	○	○	○	○	○	○	○	○	○	○	○	○	○	○	○	○	○	○	○	○	○	○	○	○	○	○	○	○	○
....	○	○	○	○	○	○	○	○	○	○	○	○	○	○	○	○	○	○	○	○	○	○	○	○	○	○	○	○	○	○	○
....	○	○	○	○	○	○	○	○	○	○	○	○	○	○	○	○	○	○	○	○	○	○	○	○	○	○	○	○	○	○	○

Habit tracker

Month: _____

This month I want to focus on:

Put a ★ for habits you can stack together.

Key: Completed ●   Partial ◐   Missed ○

Habit	1	2	3	4	5	6	7	8	9	10	11	12	13	14	15	16	17	18	19	20	21	22	23	24	25	26	27	28	29	30	31
....	○	○	○	○	○	○	○	○	○	○	○	○	○	○	○	○	○	○	○	○	○	○	○	○	○	○	○	○	○	○	○
....	○	○	○	○	○	○	○	○	○	○	○	○	○	○	○	○	○	○	○	○	○	○	○	○	○	○	○	○	○	○	○
....	○	○	○	○	○	○	○	○	○	○	○	○	○	○	○	○	○	○	○	○	○	○	○	○	○	○	○	○	○	○	○
....	○	○	○	○	○	○	○	○	○	○	○	○	○	○	○	○	○	○	○	○	○	○	○	○	○	○	○	○	○	○	○
....	○	○	○	○	○	○	○	○	○	○	○	○	○	○	○	○	○	○	○	○	○	○	○	○	○	○	○	○	○	○	○
....	○	○	○	○	○	○	○	○	○	○	○	○	○	○	○	○	○	○	○	○	○	○	○	○	○	○	○	○	○	○	○
....	○	○	○	○	○	○	○	○	○	○	○	○	○	○	○	○	○	○	○	○	○	○	○	○	○	○	○	○	○	○	○
....	○	○	○	○	○	○	○	○	○	○	○	○	○	○	○	○	○	○	○	○	○	○	○	○	○	○	○	○	○	○	○
....	○	○	○	○	○	○	○	○	○	○	○	○	○	○	○	○	○	○	○	○	○	○	○	○	○	○	○	○	○	○	○
....	○	○	○	○	○	○	○	○	○	○	○	○	○	○	○	○	○	○	○	○	○	○	○	○	○	○	○	○	○	○	○

Habit tracker

Month: _____

This month I want to focus on:

Put a ★ for habits you can stack together.

Key: Completed ● Partial ◐ Missed ○

Habit	1	2	3	4	5	6	7	8	9	10	11	12	13	14	15	16	17	18	19	20	21	22	23	24	25	26	27	28	29	30	31
	○	○	○	○	○	○	○	○	○	○	○	○	○	○	○	○	○	○	○	○	○	○	○	○	○	○	○	○	○	○	○
	○	○	○	○	○	○	○	○	○	○	○	○	○	○	○	○	○	○	○	○	○	○	○	○	○	○	○	○	○	○	○
	○	○	○	○	○	○	○	○	○	○	○	○	○	○	○	○	○	○	○	○	○	○	○	○	○	○	○	○	○	○	○
	○	○	○	○	○	○	○	○	○	○	○	○	○	○	○	○	○	○	○	○	○	○	○	○	○	○	○	○	○	○	○
	○	○	○	○	○	○	○	○	○	○	○	○	○	○	○	○	○	○	○	○	○	○	○	○	○	○	○	○	○	○	○
	○	○	○	○	○	○	○	○	○	○	○	○	○	○	○	○	○	○	○	○	○	○	○	○	○	○	○	○	○	○	○
	○	○	○	○	○	○	○	○	○	○	○	○	○	○	○	○	○	○	○	○	○	○	○	○	○	○	○	○	○	○	○
	○	○	○	○	○	○	○	○	○	○	○	○	○	○	○	○	○	○	○	○	○	○	○	○	○	○	○	○	○	○	○
	○	○	○	○	○	○	○	○	○	○	○	○	○	○	○	○	○	○	○	○	○	○	○	○	○	○	○	○	○	○	○
	○	○	○	○	○	○	○	○	○	○	○	○	○	○	○	○	○	○	○	○	○	○	○	○	○	○	○	○	○	○	○

Habit tracker

Month: _____

This month I want to focus on:

Put a ★ for habits you can stack together.

Key: Completed ● Partial ◕ Missed ○

Habit	1	2	3	4	5	6	7	8	9	10	11	12	13	14	15	16	17	18	19	20	21	22	23	24	25	26	27	28	29	30	31
....	○	○	○	○	○	○	○	○	○	○	○	○	○	○	○	○	○	○	○	○	○	○	○	○	○	○	○	○	○	○	○
....	○	○	○	○	○	○	○	○	○	○	○	○	○	○	○	○	○	○	○	○	○	○	○	○	○	○	○	○	○	○	○
....	○	○	○	○	○	○	○	○	○	○	○	○	○	○	○	○	○	○	○	○	○	○	○	○	○	○	○	○	○	○	○
....	○	○	○	○	○	○	○	○	○	○	○	○	○	○	○	○	○	○	○	○	○	○	○	○	○	○	○	○	○	○	○
....	○	○	○	○	○	○	○	○	○	○	○	○	○	○	○	○	○	○	○	○	○	○	○	○	○	○	○	○	○	○	○
....	○	○	○	○	○	○	○	○	○	○	○	○	○	○	○	○	○	○	○	○	○	○	○	○	○	○	○	○	○	○	○
....	○	○	○	○	○	○	○	○	○	○	○	○	○	○	○	○	○	○	○	○	○	○	○	○	○	○	○	○	○	○	○
....	○	○	○	○	○	○	○	○	○	○	○	○	○	○	○	○	○	○	○	○	○	○	○	○	○	○	○	○	○	○	○
....	○	○	○	○	○	○	○	○	○	○	○	○	○	○	○	○	○	○	○	○	○	○	○	○	○	○	○	○	○	○	○
....	○	○	○	○	○	○	○	○	○	○	○	○	○	○	○	○	○	○	○	○	○	○	○	○	○	○	○	○	○	○	○
....	○	○	○	○	○	○	○	○	○	○	○	○	○	○	○	○	○	○	○	○	○	○	○	○	○	○	○	○	○	○	○
....	○	○	○	○	○	○	○	○	○	○	○	○	○	○	○	○	○	○	○	○	○	○	○	○	○	○	○	○	○	○	○

Habit tracker

Month: _____

This month I want to focus on:

Put a ★ for habits you can stack together.

Key: Completed ● Partial ◗ Missed ○

Habit	1	2	3	4	5	6	7	8	9	10	11	12	13	14	15	16	17	18	19	20	21	22	23	24	25	26	27	28	29	30	31
....	○	○	○	○	○	○	○	○	○	○	○	○	○	○	○	○	○	○	○	○	○	○	○	○	○	○	○	○	○	○	○
....	○	○	○	○	○	○	○	○	○	○	○	○	○	○	○	○	○	○	○	○	○	○	○	○	○	○	○	○	○	○	○
....	○	○	○	○	○	○	○	○	○	○	○	○	○	○	○	○	○	○	○	○	○	○	○	○	○	○	○	○	○	○	○
....	○	○	○	○	○	○	○	○	○	○	○	○	○	○	○	○	○	○	○	○	○	○	○	○	○	○	○	○	○	○	○
....	○	○	○	○	○	○	○	○	○	○	○	○	○	○	○	○	○	○	○	○	○	○	○	○	○	○	○	○	○	○	○
....	○	○	○	○	○	○	○	○	○	○	○	○	○	○	○	○	○	○	○	○	○	○	○	○	○	○	○	○	○	○	○
....	○	○	○	○	○	○	○	○	○	○	○	○	○	○	○	○	○	○	○	○	○	○	○	○	○	○	○	○	○	○	○
....	○	○	○	○	○	○	○	○	○	○	○	○	○	○	○	○	○	○	○	○	○	○	○	○	○	○	○	○	○	○	○
....	○	○	○	○	○	○	○	○	○	○	○	○	○	○	○	○	○	○	○	○	○	○	○	○	○	○	○	○	○	○	○
....	○	○	○	○	○	○	○	○	○	○	○	○	○	○	○	○	○	○	○	○	○	○	○	○	○	○	○	○	○	○	○

Habit tracker

Month: _____

This month I want to focus on:

Put a ★ for habits you can stack together.

Key: Completed ● Partial ◗ Missed ○

Habit	1	2	3	4	5	6	7	8	9	10	11	12	13	14	15	16	17	18	19	20	21	22	23	24	25	26	27	28	29	30	31
....	○	○	○	○	○	○	○	○	○	○	○	○	○	○	○	○	○	○	○	○	○	○	○	○	○	○	○	○	○	○	○
....	○	○	○	○	○	○	○	○	○	○	○	○	○	○	○	○	○	○	○	○	○	○	○	○	○	○	○	○	○	○	○
....	○	○	○	○	○	○	○	○	○	○	○	○	○	○	○	○	○	○	○	○	○	○	○	○	○	○	○	○	○	○	○
....	○	○	○	○	○	○	○	○	○	○	○	○	○	○	○	○	○	○	○	○	○	○	○	○	○	○	○	○	○	○	○
....	○	○	○	○	○	○	○	○	○	○	○	○	○	○	○	○	○	○	○	○	○	○	○	○	○	○	○	○	○	○	○
....	○	○	○	○	○	○	○	○	○	○	○	○	○	○	○	○	○	○	○	○	○	○	○	○	○	○	○	○	○	○	○
....	○	○	○	○	○	○	○	○	○	○	○	○	○	○	○	○	○	○	○	○	○	○	○	○	○	○	○	○	○	○	○
....	○	○	○	○	○	○	○	○	○	○	○	○	○	○	○	○	○	○	○	○	○	○	○	○	○	○	○	○	○	○	○
....	○	○	○	○	○	○	○	○	○	○	○	○	○	○	○	○	○	○	○	○	○	○	○	○	○	○	○	○	○	○	○
....	○	○	○	○	○	○	○	○	○	○	○	○	○	○	○	○	○	○	○	○	○	○	○	○	○	○	○	○	○	○	○

Habit tracker

Month: _____

This month I want to focus on:

Put a ★ for habits you can stack together.

Key: Completed ● Partial ◐ Missed ○

Habit	1	2	3	4	5	6	7	8	9	10	11	12	13	14	15	16	17	18	19	20	21	22	23	24	25	26	27	28	29	30	31
	○	○	○	○	○	○	○	○	○	○	○	○	○	○	○	○	○	○	○	○	○	○	○	○	○	○	○	○	○	○	○
	○	○	○	○	○	○	○	○	○	○	○	○	○	○	○	○	○	○	○	○	○	○	○	○	○	○	○	○	○	○	○
	○	○	○	○	○	○	○	○	○	○	○	○	○	○	○	○	○	○	○	○	○	○	○	○	○	○	○	○	○	○	○
	○	○	○	○	○	○	○	○	○	○	○	○	○	○	○	○	○	○	○	○	○	○	○	○	○	○	○	○	○	○	○
	○	○	○	○	○	○	○	○	○	○	○	○	○	○	○	○	○	○	○	○	○	○	○	○	○	○	○	○	○	○	○
	○	○	○	○	○	○	○	○	○	○	○	○	○	○	○	○	○	○	○	○	○	○	○	○	○	○	○	○	○	○	○
	○	○	○	○	○	○	○	○	○	○	○	○	○	○	○	○	○	○	○	○	○	○	○	○	○	○	○	○	○	○	○
	○	○	○	○	○	○	○	○	○	○	○	○	○	○	○	○	○	○	○	○	○	○	○	○	○	○	○	○	○	○	○
	○	○	○	○	○	○	○	○	○	○	○	○	○	○	○	○	○	○	○	○	○	○	○	○	○	○	○	○	○	○	○
	○	○	○	○	○	○	○	○	○	○	○	○	○	○	○	○	○	○	○	○	○	○	○	○	○	○	○	○	○	○	○
	○	○	○	○	○	○	○	○	○	○	○	○	○	○	○	○	○	○	○	○	○	○	○	○	○	○	○	○	○	○	○
	○	○	○	○	○	○	○	○	○	○	○	○	○	○	○	○	○	○	○	○	○	○	○	○	○	○	○	○	○	○	○
	○	○	○	○	○	○	○	○	○	○	○	○	○	○	○	○	○	○	○	○	○	○	○	○	○	○	○	○	○	○	○

Habit tracker

Month: _____

This month I want to focus on:

Put a ★ for habits you can stack together.

Key: Completed ● Partial ◗ Missed ○

Habit	1	2	3	4	5	6	7	8	9	10	11	12	13	14	15	16	17	18	19	20	21	22	23	24	25	26	27	28	29	30	31
	○	○	○	○	○	○	○	○	○	○	○	○	○	○	○	○	○	○	○	○	○	○	○	○	○	○	○	○	○	○	○
	○	○	○	○	○	○	○	○	○	○	○	○	○	○	○	○	○	○	○	○	○	○	○	○	○	○	○	○	○	○	○
	○	○	○	○	○	○	○	○	○	○	○	○	○	○	○	○	○	○	○	○	○	○	○	○	○	○	○	○	○	○	○
	○	○	○	○	○	○	○	○	○	○	○	○	○	○	○	○	○	○	○	○	○	○	○	○	○	○	○	○	○	○	○
	○	○	○	○	○	○	○	○	○	○	○	○	○	○	○	○	○	○	○	○	○	○	○	○	○	○	○	○	○	○	○
	○	○	○	○	○	○	○	○	○	○	○	○	○	○	○	○	○	○	○	○	○	○	○	○	○	○	○	○	○	○	○
	○	○	○	○	○	○	○	○	○	○	○	○	○	○	○	○	○	○	○	○	○	○	○	○	○	○	○	○	○	○	○
	○	○	○	○	○	○	○	○	○	○	○	○	○	○	○	○	○	○	○	○	○	○	○	○	○	○	○	○	○	○	○
	○	○	○	○	○	○	○	○	○	○	○	○	○	○	○	○	○	○	○	○	○	○	○	○	○	○	○	○	○	○	○
	○	○	○	○	○	○	○	○	○	○	○	○	○	○	○	○	○	○	○	○	○	○	○	○	○	○	○	○	○	○	○
	○	○	○	○	○	○	○	○	○	○	○	○	○	○	○	○	○	○	○	○	○	○	○	○	○	○	○	○	○	○	○
	○	○	○	○	○	○	○	○	○	○	○	○	○	○	○	○	○	○	○	○	○	○	○	○	○	○	○	○	○	○	○

Habit tracker

Month: _____

This month I want to focus on:

Put a ★ for habits you can stack together.

Key: Completed ● Partial ◑ Missed ○

Habit	1	2	3	4	5	6	7	8	9	10	11	12	13	14	15	16	17	18	19	20	21	22	23	24	25	26	27	28	29	30	31
	○	○	○	○	○	○	○	○	○	○	○	○	○	○	○	○	○	○	○	○	○	○	○	○	○	○	○	○	○	○	○
	○	○	○	○	○	○	○	○	○	○	○	○	○	○	○	○	○	○	○	○	○	○	○	○	○	○	○	○	○	○	○
	○	○	○	○	○	○	○	○	○	○	○	○	○	○	○	○	○	○	○	○	○	○	○	○	○	○	○	○	○	○	○
	○	○	○	○	○	○	○	○	○	○	○	○	○	○	○	○	○	○	○	○	○	○	○	○	○	○	○	○	○	○	○
	○	○	○	○	○	○	○	○	○	○	○	○	○	○	○	○	○	○	○	○	○	○	○	○	○	○	○	○	○	○	○
	○	○	○	○	○	○	○	○	○	○	○	○	○	○	○	○	○	○	○	○	○	○	○	○	○	○	○	○	○	○	○
	○	○	○	○	○	○	○	○	○	○	○	○	○	○	○	○	○	○	○	○	○	○	○	○	○	○	○	○	○	○	○
	○	○	○	○	○	○	○	○	○	○	○	○	○	○	○	○	○	○	○	○	○	○	○	○	○	○	○	○	○	○	○
	○	○	○	○	○	○	○	○	○	○	○	○	○	○	○	○	○	○	○	○	○	○	○	○	○	○	○	○	○	○	○
	○	○	○	○	○	○	○	○	○	○	○	○	○	○	○	○	○	○	○	○	○	○	○	○	○	○	○	○	○	○	○

Monthly planner & goal setting

Setting realistic but meaty goals each month will help keep you focused. To make each goal achievable, you can break it down into smaller, more granular goals. For example, maybe you want to complete a *Michel Thomas Method* audio course. You can set yourself a mini goal such as "Listen to 30 minutes every day on my commute." Make sure you reward yourself for each of your wins. To help you stay motivated, I provide some tips and missions each month that you can use when you need a boost.

Wenye macho huona; lakini mwenye hamu hutafuta

Having a dream is more important than having your eyes.

or

Dream big.

Swahili idiom

My goals

Month: _____

Focus word of the month: _____

Monthly goal:	How did you do?

Breakdown   Completed?

1 ....   ◯

2 ....   ◯

3 ....   ◯

Rewards   Earned?

1 ....   ◯

2 ....   ◯

3 ....   ◯

Learning tip

Find an accountability partner or study buddy and start a weekly check-in with them, scheduling it on your calendar to stay on top of your goals. Try to write and speak to each other only in your target language.

Mission

Introduce yourself in your target language and film it to capture your "before." You've got this, mistakes and all!

Monthly planner

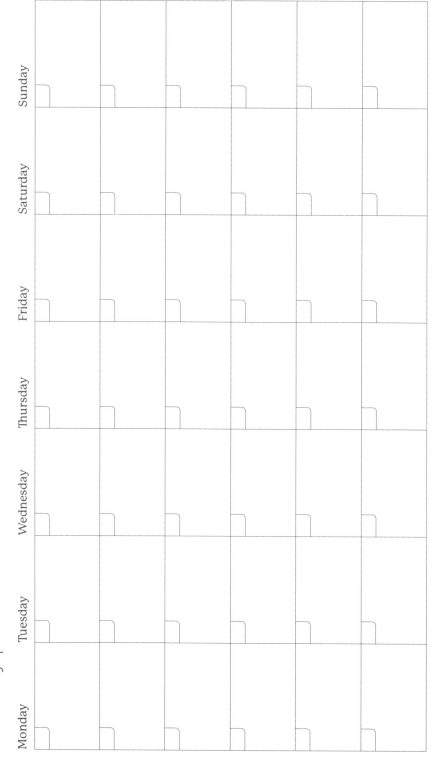

Monday | Tuesday | Wednesday | Thursday | Friday | Saturday | Sunday

My goals

Month: _____

Focus word of the month: _____

Monthly goal:	How did you do?

Breakdown   Completed?

1 .... ○

2 .... ○

3 .... ○

Rewards   Earned?

1 .... ○

2 .... ○

3 .... ○

Learning tip

Commit to 5 minutes a day of studying your language. Whether it's writing a journal entry, reading a short story, or listening to a podcast, you'll feel like you've accomplished something.

Mission

Find an Instagram account in your target language—stalk it, learn, follow, and repeat.

Monthly planner

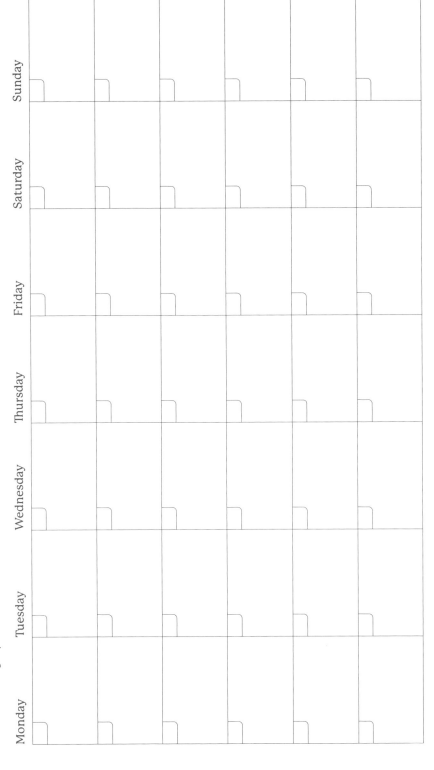

Monday | Tuesday | Wednesday | Thursday | Friday | Saturday | Sunday

My goals

Focus word of the month: _____

Monthly goal:	How did you do?

Breakdown   Completed?

1 ....   ◯

2 ....   ◯

3 ....   ◯

Rewards   Earned?

1 ....   ◯

2 ....   ◯

3 ....   ◯

Learning tip

Consistency Habit stack like a pro by making your language learning more efficient. If you work out every day, listen to music in your target language. If you wash dishes daily, take an audio lesson while rinsing. Language learning is time consuming, so be strategic.

Mission

Do a workout class in your target language— yoga, breathing, and meditation count!

Monthly planner

Monday	Tuesday	Wednesday	Thursday	Friday	Saturday	Sunday

My goals

Month: _____

Focus word of the month: _____

Monthly goal:	How did you do?

Breakdown   Completed?

1 ....   ◯

2 ....   ◯

3 ....   ◯

Rewards   Earned?

1 ....   ◯

2 ....   ◯

3 ....   ◯

Learning tip

Accountability My favorite way to retain information is to teach it to someone else. Grab your accountability buddy and divide and conquer: Each of you studies a complicated list of vocabulary or verb tense and take turns teaching the other.

Mission

Identify what you're struggling with and spend 30 minutes focusing on just that.

Monthly planner

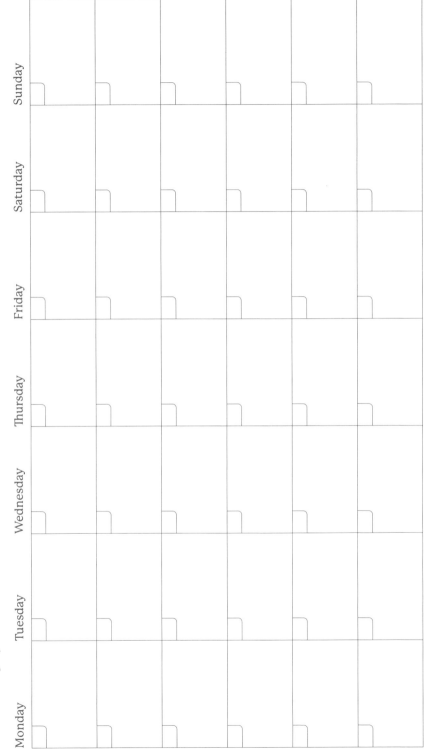

Monday	Tuesday	Wednesday	Thursday	Friday	Saturday	Sunday

My goals

Month: _____

Focus word of the month: _____

Monthly goal:	How did you do?

Breakdown   Completed?

1 .... ○

2 .... ○

3 .... ○

Rewards   Earned?

1 .... ○

2 .... ○

3 .... ○

Learning tip

Vocabulary Embrace cognates and identify those tricky words known as false friends. Make a list of all the words that are the same in both your target and first language. Take note of any false friends. Keep a comparison chart and refer to it as often as possible.

Mission

Find and make a recipe in your target language. Make a note of any new vocabulary in your journal.

Monthly planner

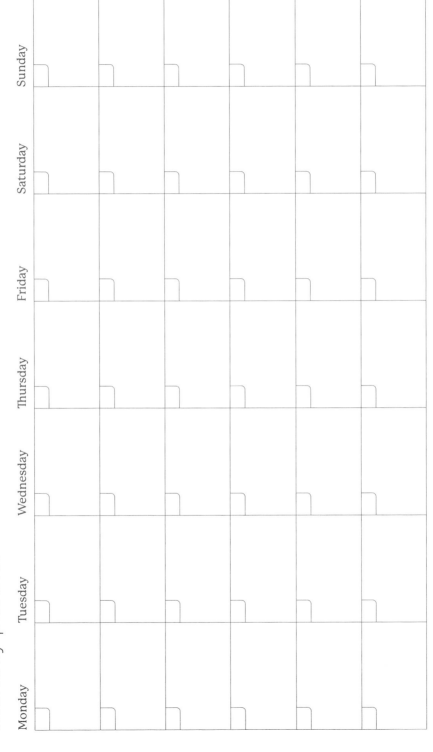

Monday	Tuesday	Wednesday	Thursday	Friday	Saturday	Sunday

My goals

Month: _____

Focus word of the month: _____

Monthly goal:	How did you do?

Breakdown   Completed?

1 .... ◯

2 .... ◯

3 .... ◯

Rewards   Earned?

1 .... ◯

2 .... ◯

3 .... ◯

Learning tip

Listening & Speaking Pause and repeat over and over again until you've absorbed what has been said, then transcribe what you've heard with paper and pen to form a mind–body connection. Read it out loud and try to match your pronunciation to the native speaker's.

Mission

Create and listen to a playlist with 10 songs in your target language.

Monthly planner

Monday	Tuesday	Wednesday	Thursday	Friday	Saturday	Sunday

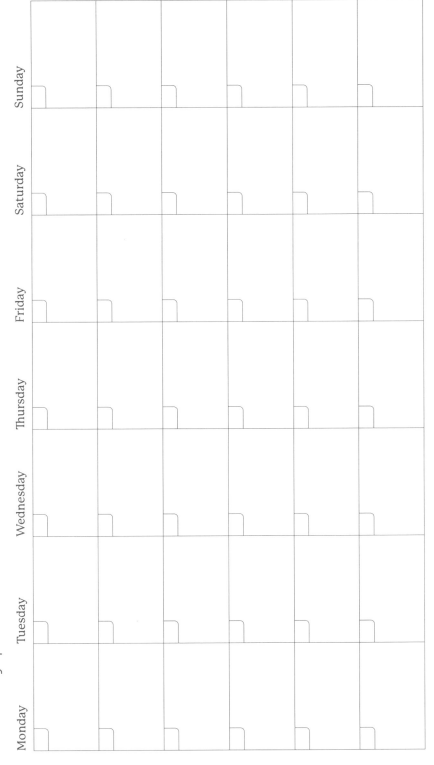

My goals

Focus word of the month: _____

Monthly goal:	How did you do?

Breakdown   Completed?

1 .... ○

2 .... ○

3 .... ○

Rewards   Earned?

1 .... ○

2 .... ○

3 .... ○

Learning tip

Comprehension Watch a TV series you've already watched in your mother tongue in your target language. Since you already understand the plot, you can focus on listening to how native speakers express themselves.

Mission

Find a TV show in your target language and write down 10 new expressions from the first episode.

Monthly planner

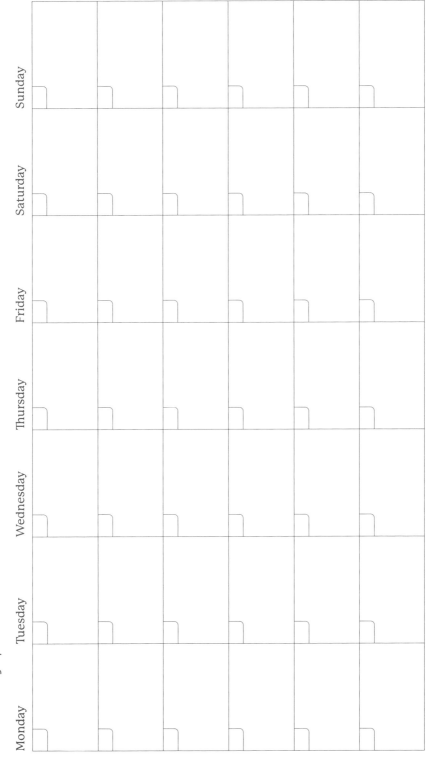

Monday	Tuesday	Wednesday	Thursday	Friday	Saturday	Sunday

My goals

Focus word of the month: _____

Monthly goal:	How did you do?

Breakdown   Completed?

1 .... ◯

2 .... ◯

3 .... ◯

Rewards   Earned?

1 .... ◯

2 .... ◯

3 .... ◯

Learning tip

Memory Create silly mnemonic devices to remember words or rules you're struggling with. Use outrageous phrases, rhymes, acronyms, or anything else that will spark your memory.

Mission

Read or listen to your target language for 10 minutes a day for one week.

Monthly planner

Monday	Tuesday	Wednesday	Thursday	Friday	Saturday	Sunday

My goals

Focus word of the month: _____

Monthly goal:	How did you do?

Breakdown   Completed?

1 .... ○

2 .... ○

3 .... ○

Rewards   Earned?

1 .... ○

2 .... ○

3 .... ○

Learning tip

Motivation Create a "studygram" on Instagram or TikTok to track your progress, meet likeminded language learners, and build an audience to keep you accountable. Plus, you'll have key moments in your language learning journey documented. Nothing lights a fire under your booty to study like your own progress.

Mission

Make a vision board in your target language of what life will look like with your newfound fluency.

Monthly planner

Monday	Tuesday	Wednesday	Thursday	Friday	Saturday	Sunday

My goals

Focus word of the month: _____

Monthly goal:	How did you do?

MONTHLY PLANNER

Breakdown   Completed?

1 .... ◯

2 .... ◯

3 .... ◯

Rewards   Earned?

1 .... ◯

2 .... ◯

3 .... ◯

Learning tip

Reading In several studies, reading materials aloud has been shown to improve memory and assist in long-term recall. Read your material out loud and record it on your phone so you can play it back and watch for your pronunciation. Share it if you feel brave!

Mission

Read one of your journal entries and film your progress.

Monthly planner

Monday	Tuesday	Wednesday	Thursday	Friday	Saturday	Sunday

My goals

Month: _____

Focus word of the month: _____

Monthly goal:	How did you do?

MONTHLY PLANNER

Breakdown   Completed?

1 .... ○

2 .... ○

3 .... ○

Rewards   Earned?

1 .... ○

2 .... ○

3 .... ○

Learning tip

Speaking Observe locals—how they speak, their filler words, how they express curiosity—and start gathering your database of expressions to develop your own interaction style. When you learn a language, it's not just *what* you say, but *how* you say it that makes you fluent*ish*.

Mission

Try to meet some native speakers IRL. Look for language exchange events or cultural organizations near your home.

Monthly planner

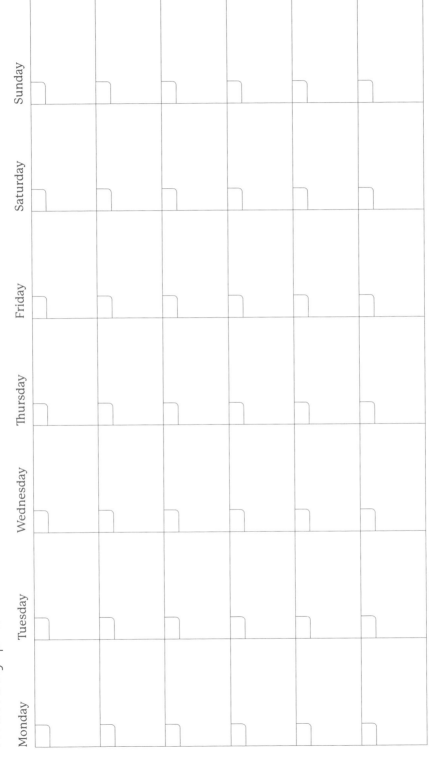

Monday | Tuesday | Wednesday | Thursday | Friday | Saturday | Sunday

My goals

Focus word of the month: _____

Monthly goal:	How did you do?

Breakdown   Completed?

1 .... ◯

2 .... ◯

3 .... ◯

Rewards   Earned?

1 .... ◯

2 .... ◯

3 .... ◯

Learning tip

Memory When learning a new list of vocabulary (including expressions and even verbs!), make a short story or write a journal entry using all of the new language. Create context that's relevant to your life so your brain starts absorbing the material. (Make sure to include the article if it's a gendered language.)

Mission

Memorize a verse in a song you love in your target language. Note any new vocabulary in your journal.

Monthly planner

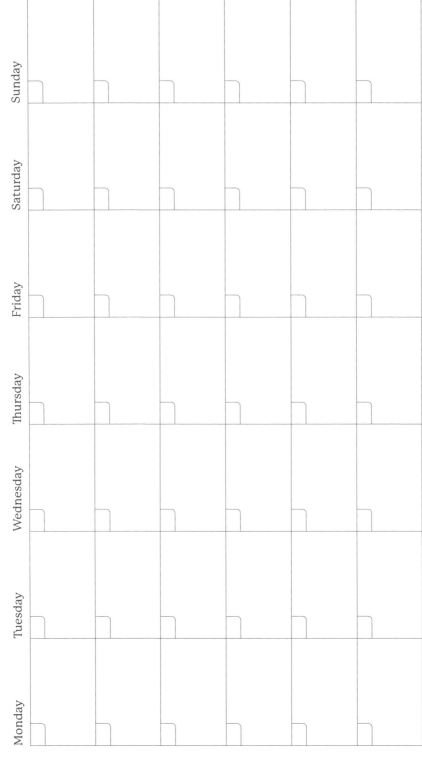

Monday | Tuesday | Wednesday | Thursday | Friday | Saturday | Sunday

Monthly self-assessment & check-in

Learning is not just about studying. It's a mind—body experience. You need to focus and to carve time out for your language learning. So what can help you? A good night's sleep? Plenty of water and taking your daily vitamin? Exercise? In this section, you want to keep track of the big picture. How is your motivation? Are you energized? Is your brain getting enough fuel? Do you feel like you're making progress? This section gives you a few ideas of the things you might want to track here. Start by adding important aspects relating to your wellbeing and take note of what you think is important to track. Then, come back here to check in on your progress each month and add something new to the list.

Monthly self-assessment

✗ = Disagree **☺** = Not really **☺** = Feeling good **★** = Absolutely

	Jan	Feb	Mar	Apr	May	Jun	Jul	Aug	Sep	Oct	Nov	Dec

Add your own measures. Think about what adjustments you want to make, who you want to connect with and, what you have learned about yourself.

Monthly check-in

What adjustments would you like to make?

Month	Response

What are you most proud of? What is your biggest win?

Month	Response

What connections have you made? Ideas for next month?

Month	Response
. . . .	. . . .
. . . .	. . . .
. . . .	. . . .
. . . .	. . . .
. . . .	. . . .
. . . .	. . . .
. . . .	. . . .
. . . .	. . . .
. . . .	. . . .
. . . .	. . . .

What have you learned about yourself?

Month	Response
. . . .	. . . .
. . . .	. . . .
. . . .	. . . .
. . . .	. . . .
. . . .	. . . .
. . . .	. . . .
. . . .	. . . .
. . . .	. . . .
. . . .	. . . .
. . . .	. . . .

Workspace

As a scrappy learner, I have always needed lots of scrap paper. I've designed this section for you to go wild. Draw your visual aids or write out a word five times. In the Workspace you have the freedom to take notes in the way you learn best. I typically write in this section during my tutoring sessions, or when I'm listening to or reading content I don't understand fully (yet).

To stay organized, be sure to add the resources you're using and write the date and location of your writing—you'll want this context to track your progress. Once you fill the Workspace pages, I suggest going back to transfer your essential learning to the highlights section; this is the content digestion that will make the learning stick. On the right side, you can take note of any questions you still have or words you want to look up. Curious students are more engaged students.

Tyvestä puuhun noustaan.

Learn to walk before you can run.

Finnish idiom

Resources:

Highlights:

Notes

Questions and practice:

Resources:

Highlights:

Notes

Questions and practice:

Resources:

Date: _____

Location: _____

Highlights:

Notes

Questions and practice:

Resources:

Date: _____

Location: _____

Highlights:

Notes

WORKSPACE

Questions and practice:

Resources:

Highlights:

Notes

Questions and practice:

Resources:

Date: _____

Location: _____

Highlights:

Notes

Questions and practice:

Resources:

Highlights:

Notes

Questions and practice:

Resources:

Highlights:

Notes

Questions and practice:

Resources:

Highlights:

Notes

Questions and practice:

Resources:

Date: _____

Location: _____

Highlights:

Notes

Questions and practice:

Resources:

Highlights:

Notes

Questions and practice:

Resources:

Highlights:

Notes

Questions and practice:

Resources:

Date: _____

Location: _____

Highlights:

Notes

Questions and practice:

Resources:

Highlights:

Notes

Questions and practice:

Resources:

Highlights:

Notes

Questions and practice:

Resources:

Date: _____

Location: _____

Highlights:

Notes

Questions and practice:

Resources:

Highlights:

Notes

WORKSPACE

Questions and practice:

Resources:

Date: _____

Location: _____

Highlights:

Notes

Questions and practice:

Resources:

Highlights:

Notes

WORKSPACE

Questions and practice:

Resources:

Date: _____

Location: _____

Highlights:

Notes

Questions and practice:

Resources:

Highlights:

Notes

Questions and practice:

Resources:

Highlights:

Notes

Questions and practice:

Resources:

Highlights:

Notes

Questions and practice:

Resources:

Highlights:

Notes

Questions and practice:

Resources:

Date: _____

Location: _____

Highlights:

Notes

Questions and practice:

Resources:

Date: _____

Location: _____

Highlights:

Notes

WORKSPACE

Questions and practice:

New language

Depending on what kind of learner you are, this section might be the most or least exciting! Regardless, seasoned language learners know it's the dry stuff that really makes the knowledge stick. Use this section to make sure you're not missing key elements that are essential to your vocabulary. From adverbs, to prepositions and conjunctions, to nouns and pronouns, this is where the building blocks of your fluency will live. My personal favorite is making a "street speak" list of all the things you'd never learn in a textbook. Grammar is grueling but necessary. To help make sense of it, it's important to find examples for rules and write notes that make them clear to you.

Pro tip: *I encourage you to find joy in verb conjugations. Use color, make doodles, do whatever it takes to keep growing your knowledge of verbs and verb tenses.*

猿も木から落ちる。
Saru mo ki kara ochiru.

Even monkeys fall from trees.
or
Everyone makes mistakes.

Japanese idiom

New vocabulary & expressions

New language	Translation/Example sentence

New language | Translation/Example sentence

New vocabulary & expressions

New language	Translation/Example sentence

New language	Translation/Example sentence

New vocabulary & expressions

New language	Translation/Example sentence

New language	Translation/Example sentence

New vocabulary & expressions

New language	Translation/Example sentence

New language	Translation/Example sentence

New vocabulary & expressions

New language	Translation/Example sentence

New language   Translation/Example sentence

New vocabulary & expressions

New language	Translation/Example sentence

New language	Translation/Example sentence

New vocabulary & expressions

New language	Translation/Example sentence

New language	Translation/Example sentence

New vocabulary & expressions

New language	Translation/Example sentence

New language	Translation/Example sentence

Verb conjugations

Infinitive: .... Meaning: ....

Verb form/Tense: .... Usage notes: ....

Infinitive: .... Meaning: ....

Verb form/Tense: .... Usage notes: ....

Infinitive: .... Meaning: ....

Verb form/Tense: .... Usage notes: ....

Infinitive: ....

Verb form/Tense: ....

Meaning: ....

Usage notes: ....

Infinitive: ....

Verb form/Tense: ....

Meaning: ....

Usage notes: ....

Infinitive: ....

Verb form/Tense: ....

Meaning: ....

Usage notes: ....

Verb conjugations

Infinitive: ....   Meaning: ....

Verb form/Tense: ....   Usage notes: ....

Infinitive: ....   Meaning: ....

Verb form/Tense: ....   Usage notes: ....

Infinitive: ....   Meaning: ....

Verb form/Tense: ....   Usage notes: ....

Infinitive: .... Meaning: ....

Verb form/Tense: .... Usage notes: ....

Infinitive: .... Meaning: ....

Verb form/Tense: .... Usage notes: ....

Infinitive: .... Meaning: ....

Verb form/Tense: .... Usage notes: ....

Verb conjugations

Infinitive: . . . . Meaning: . . . .

Verb form/Tense: . . . . Usage notes: . . . .

Infinitive: . . . . Meaning: . . . .

Verb form/Tense: . . . . Usage notes: . . . .

Infinitive: . . . . Meaning: . . . .

Verb form/Tense: . . . . Usage notes: . . . .

Infinitive: .... Meaning: ....

Verb form/Tense: .... Usage notes: ....

Infinitive: .... Meaning: ....

Verb form/Tense: .... Usage notes: ....

Infinitive: .... Meaning: ....

Verb form/Tense: .... Usage notes: ....

Verb conjugations

Infinitive: . . . .   Meaning: . . . .

Verb form/Tense: . . . .   Usage notes: . . . .

Infinitive: . . . .   Meaning: . . . .

Verb form/Tense: . . . .   Usage notes: . . . .

Infinitive: . . . .   Meaning: . . . .

Verb form/Tense: . . . .   Usage notes: . . . .

Infinitive: ....

Meaning: ....

Verb form/Tense: ....

Usage notes: ....

....

....

....

....

....

....

....

....

....

....

Infinitive: ....

Meaning: ....

Verb form/Tense: ....

Usage notes: ....

....

....

....

....

....

....

....

....

....

....

Infinitive: ....

Meaning: ....

Verb form/Tense: ....

Usage notes: ....

....

....

....

....

....

....

....

....

....

....

Verb conjugations

Infinitive: .... Meaning: ....

Verb form/Tense: .... Usage notes: ....

Infinitive: .... Meaning: ....

Verb form/Tense: .... Usage notes: ....

Infinitive: .... Meaning: ....

Verb form/Tense: .... Usage notes: ....

Infinitive: Meaning:

Verb form/Tense: Usage notes:

Infinitive: Meaning:

Verb form/Tense: Usage notes:

Infinitive: Meaning:

Verb form/Tense: Usage notes:

Verb conjugations

Infinitive: . . . . Meaning: . . . .

Verb form/Tense: . . . . Usage notes: . . . .

Infinitive: . . . . Meaning: . . . .

Verb form/Tense: . . . . Usage notes: . . . .

Infinitive: . . . . Meaning: . . . .

Verb form/Tense: . . . . Usage notes: . . . .

Infinitive: . . . . Meaning: . . . .

Verb form/Tense: . . . . Usage notes: . . . .

Infinitive: . . . . Meaning: . . . .

Verb form/Tense: . . . . Usage notes: . . . .

Infinitive: . . . . Meaning: . . . .

Verb form/Tense: . . . . Usage notes: . . . .

Verb conjugations

Infinitive: ....

Meaning: ....

Verb form/Tense: ....

Usage notes: ....

Infinitive: ....

Meaning: ....

Verb form/Tense: ....

Usage notes: ....

Infinitive: ....

Meaning: ....

Verb form/Tense: ....

Usage notes: ....

Infinitive: .... Meaning: ....

Verb form/Tense: .... Usage notes: ....

Infinitive: .... Meaning: ....

Verb form/Tense: .... Usage notes: ....

Infinitive: .... Meaning: ....

Verb form/Tense: .... Usage notes: ....

Verb conjugations

Infinitive: .... Meaning: ....

Verb form/Tense: .... Usage notes: ....

Infinitive: .... Meaning: ....

Verb form/Tense: .... Usage notes: ....

Infinitive: .... Meaning: ....

Verb form/Tense: .... Usage notes: ....

Infinitive: .... Meaning: ....

Verb form/Tense: .... Usage notes: ....

Infinitive: .... Meaning: ....

Verb form/Tense: .... Usage notes: ....

Infinitive: .... Meaning: ....

Verb form/Tense: .... Usage notes: ....

Grammar rules

Rule/Structure	Example/Usage notes

Rule/Structure	Example/Usage notes

Grammar rules

Rule/Structure	Example/Usage notes

Rule/Structure	Example/Usage notes

Grammar rules

Rule/Structure	Example/Usage notes

Rule/Structure	Example/Usage notes

Grammar rules

Rule/Structure

Example/Usage notes

Rule/Structure	Example/Usage notes

Rule/Structure	Example/Usage notes

Grammar rules

Rule/Structure	Example/Usage notes

Rule/Structure	Example/Usage notes

Grammar rules

Rule/Structure	Example/Usage notes

Rule/Structure	Example/Usage notes

Grammar rules

Rule/Structure	Example/Usage notes

Rule/Structure	Example/Usage notes

Prompts

In 2020 I founded a journaling company,
JoClub, where I've mastered the art
of asking deep questions to unlock
perspectives that would otherwise
never come to the surface. As a
language learner, I started translating
and answering prompts to sharpen my
Greek skills, and to help me have more
dynamic discussions with French, Italian,
Brazilian, and Spanish friends. After a
few days of consistent journaling, I was
shocked at how much I had retained and
loved how fun it was.

There is scientific evidence that proves we unlock
diverse ways of thinking if we use different
languages. Here's a mini challenge for you:
Answer the same prompt in two languages and
see what happens. Research says your mother
tongue is associated with more emotional ways of
thinking, while your secondary language will be
more logical.

   In other words, we can hack our brains by
being fluent*ish*!

These prompts are written to elicit language appropriate for your level, but you can choose your prompt according to what you want to write about that day. As you progress in your language, so will your thoughts and ideas. The higher-level prompts are slightly more introspective and philosophical, while the beginner prompts deal more with everyday life. I challenge you to push yourself to incorporate different verb tenses and new idioms or expressions as you build your journaling habit. Try formal writing and informal writing. And, of course, if you're feeling inspired, create your own prompt, answer it, and share it with a friend.

Beginner

Prompt	Date	Page #
1. How are you feeling today?		
2. Write about your family.		
3. Where do you live? What do you (not) love about it?		
4. What do you do for work? Why do you do it?		
5. Write a letter to a friend you haven't seen in a while. Explain to them how you're doing.		
6. What is your favorite part of the day? Why?		
7. What is your favorite holiday?		
8. Where do you like to go when you're stressed?		
9. What's your favorite meal?		
10. How do you like to stay active?		
11. Write about someone who is important to you, and why.		
12. What is your favorite genre of music? Why?		
13. Describe your morning routine.		
14. Describe your night routine.		
15. What is your favorite season? Why?		
16. What do you do to relax?		
17. Write about your favorite film.		
18. Write about someone you admire.		
19. Write about your friendship group.		
20. Why are you learning a new language?		
21. What did you do last weekend?		
22. What is your favorite aspect of yourself?		
23. What is your goal for your target language?		
24. How does journaling benefit you?		
25. What's one thing about yourself that you want to improve?		
26. Write about your dream job or retirement.		
27. What is your dream holiday?		

Intermediate

Prompt	Date	Page #
1. Write about your favorite art form. Why do you connect to it?		
2. Are you disciplined? Why/why not?		
3. Do you procrastinate more than you would like to?		
4. What advice would you give yourself 5 years ago?		
5. Write a letter to yourself in 5 years.		
6. Do you feel you have a good balance in your life? What is off-balance?		
7. What is being neglected that you consider important?		
8. Write about your relationship with failure.		
9. Write about your relationship with success.		
10. What do you do to keep your mind healthy?		
11. What do you do to keep your body healthy?		
12. What lesson have you learned about life this month?		
13. When was the last time you felt wonder?		
14. What is your favorite quality about yourself in this new language?		
15. Do you treat yourself regularly? In what ways?		
16. How do you want people to remember you?		
17. How would a friend or loved one describe you if you weren't there?		
18. Write about something or someone you couldn't live without.		
19. What are your main core values? Why are they important to you?		
20. What actions do you take daily that demonstrate your values?		
21. Write about your relationship with pride.		
22. What traits do your favorite people have in common?		
23. Are you often harsh on yourself when you make mistakes?		

Prompt	Date	Page #
24. What impression do you leave on people when you walk into a room?		
25. How would people's impression of you change after spending more time with you?		
26. What would people say about you when you're not in the room?		
27. What is the best piece of advice you've ever gotten? Do you still follow it?		
28. Describe a time you felt fully engaged and alive.		
29. What do you need to let go of to make space for something greater?		

Advanced

Prompt	Date	Page #
1. Describe passion and the different ways it shows up in your life.		
2. Who or what influences your decisions? Your internal compass or external factors?		
3. What are you grateful for this year or the past year?		
4. Write about all the things you want to remember from the past month.		
5. What do you want your life to look like in a year's time?		
6. Write about an early job. How did it influence your character today		
7. What habits do you love maintaining? What habits do you want to cultivate?		
8. Write about your life from the perspective of your ideal self 10 years from now.		
9. Do you treat yourself with the same respect that you treat your loved ones?		
10. Write in detail about the happiest time of your life.		
11. Write about three moments in your life that changed how you see the world.		
12. What's the best piece of advice you ever heard? Do you still follow it?		

Prompt	Date	Page #
13. What is an opinion you have that others might disagree with?		
14. Describe what character you would be if you were in a movie.		
15. Who will you be in this new language?		
16. What is your relationship with silence? Does it make you comfortable or uncomfortable?		
17. What is your favorite character trait that you have? How has it served you?		
18. What patterns are no longer serving you from childhood?		
19. What habits from childhood do you still incorporate into your adult life?		
20. What advice would you give yourself if you were your own friend?		
21. If you had known where you'd be now 10 years ago, what would you have changed? What would you have done the same?		
22. Write about your relationship with change. Do you embrace or resist it?		
23. What would your life look like if you didn't have access to technology?		
24. Describe your most fulfilling life in all aspects (financial, social, career, home life, love, family, etc.).		
25. Write about your relationship with regret.		
26. What legacy do you want to leave behind?		
27. If you could teach anyone one thing, what would it be and why?		
28. What would your younger self think of where you are today?		
29. What advice would your older self give you?		
30. How do you want your life to evolve with this new language and identity?		

Journal

This is where the magic happens.

I've designed this section to help you develop your personality in your new language, as well as your language skills. The more you journal, the easier and more interesting it gets. In this section you'll start expressing yourself in your target language by answering thought-provoking questions that can be used in real-life scenarios.

My favorite part about journaling, regardless of the language, is that it's a receipt of your evolution, an investment in your relationship with yourself, and a tool for mental wellness. You'll be able to read what you wrote as a spectator to your own life, and see your fluency grow, page by page.

Pro tip: *Be sure to look up the words and phrases you need with online translators and cross-reference your sources.*

Petit à petit, l'oiseau fait son nid.

Little by little the bird
makes its nest.

or

Take things step by step.

French idiom

Prompt #: ____ Date: _____ Location: _____

Prompt or prompt translation:

JOURNAL

New language:

Translation:

Prompt #: ___   Date: _____   Location: _____

Prompt or prompt translation:

New language: Translation:

Prompt or prompt translation:

New language: Translation:

Prompt #: ___ Date: _____ Location: _____

Prompt or prompt translation:

New language: Translation:

Prompt or prompt translation:

New language:

Translation:

JOURNAL

Prompt #: ___ Date: _____ Location: _____

Prompt or prompt translation:

....
....
....
....
....
....
....
....
....
....
....
....
....
....
....
....

JOURNAL

New language: Translation:

....
....
....
....
....
....
....

Prompt #: ___ Date: _____ Location: _____

Prompt or prompt translation:

New language: **Translation:**

Prompt #: ___ Date: _____ Location: _____

Prompt or prompt translation:

....
....
....
....
....
....
....
....
....
....
....
....
....
....
....

New language: **Translation:**

....
....
....
....
....
....
....

Prompt #: ___ Date: _____ Location: _____

Prompt or prompt translation:

....
....
....
....
....
....
....
....
....
....
....
....
....
....
....

New language: **Translation:**

....
....
....
....
....
....

Prompt #: ___ Date: _____ Location: _____

Prompt or prompt translation:

....

....

....

....

....

....

....

....

....

....

....

....

....

....

....

....

....

JOURNAL

New language: Translation:

....

....

....

....

....

....

....

Prompt or prompt translation:

JOURNAL

New language:

Translation:

Prompt or prompt translation:

New language: Translation:

Prompt #: ___   Date: _____   Location: _____

Prompt or prompt translation:

Prompt #: ___   Date: _____   Location: _____

Prompt or prompt translation:

Prompt #: ___ Date: _____ Location: _____

Prompt or prompt translation:

Prompt #: ___ Date: _____ Location: _____

Prompt or prompt translation:

Prompt or prompt translation:

Prompt #: ___ Date: _____ Location: _____

Prompt or prompt translation:

Prompt #: ___ Date: _____ Location: _____

Prompt or prompt translation:

Prompt #: ___ Date: _____ Location: _____

Prompt or prompt translation:

JOURNAL

Prompt or prompt translation:

JOURNAL

Prompt #: ___   Date: _____   Location: _____

Prompt or prompt translation:

Prompt #: ___ Date: _____ Location: _____

Prompt or prompt translation:

Prompt #: ___ Date: _____ Location: _____

Prompt or prompt translation:

Prompt or prompt translation:

JOURNAL

Prompt #: ___ Date: _____ Location: _____

Prompt or prompt translation:

Prompt or prompt translation:

Prompt #: ___ Date: _____ Location: _____

Prompt or prompt translation:

Prompt #: ___ Date: _____ Location: _____

Prompt or prompt translation:

JOURNAL

194

Prompt #: ___ Date: _____ Location: _____

Prompt or prompt translation:

Prompt or prompt translation:

JOURNAL

Prompt #: _____ Date: _____ Location: _____

Prompt or prompt translation:

JOURNAL

Prompt #: ___ Date: _____ Location: _____

Prompt or prompt translation:

....
....
....
....
....
....
....
....
....
....
....
....
....
....
....
....
....
....
....
....
....
....
....

JOURNAL

Prompt #: ___ Date: _____ Location: _____

Prompt or prompt translation:

Prompt #: ___ Date: _____ Location: _____

Prompt or prompt translation:

Prompt #: ___ Date: _____ Location: _____

Prompt or prompt translation:

Prompt #: ___ Date: _____ Location: _____

Prompt or prompt translation:

JOURNAL

Prompt #: ___ Date: _____ Location: _____

Prompt or prompt translation:

Prompt or prompt translation:

Prompt #: ___ Date: _____ Location: _____

Prompt or prompt translation:

Prompt #: ___ Date: _____ Location: _____

Prompt or prompt translation:

Prompt #: ___ Date: _____ Location: _____

Prompt or prompt translation:

Prompt #: ___ Date: _____ Location: _____

Prompt or prompt translation:

JOURNAL

Prompt #: ___ Date: _____ Location: _____

Prompt or prompt translation:

JOURNAL

Prompt or prompt translation:

Prompt or prompt translation:

Prompt #: ___ Date: _____ Location: _____

Prompt or prompt translation:

Prompt #: ___ Date: _____ Location: _____

Prompt or prompt translation:

Prompt or prompt translation:

Prompt #: ___ Date: _____ Location: _____

Prompt or prompt translation:

Prompt or prompt translation:

JOURNAL

Prompt #: ___   Date: _____   Location: _____

Prompt or prompt translation:

Prompt or prompt translation:

Prompt #: ___   Date: _____   Location: _____

Prompt or prompt translation:

....

....

....

....

....

....

....

....

....

....

....

....

....

....

....

....

....

....

....

....

....

....

....

....

JOURNAL

Prompt #: ___   Date: _____   Location: _____

Prompt or prompt translation:

Prompt #: ___   Date: _____   Location: _____

Prompt or prompt translation:

Prompt #: ___ Date: _____ Location: _____

Prompt or prompt translation:

Prompt #: ___ Date: _____ Location: _____

Prompt or prompt translation:

Prompt or prompt translation:

Prompt #: ___ Date: _____ Location: _____

Prompt or prompt translation:

JOURNAL

Prompt or prompt translation:

Prompt #: ___ Date: _____ Location: _____

Prompt or prompt translation:

Prompt #: ___   Date: _____   Location: _____

Prompt or prompt translation:

JOURNAL

Prompt #: ___ Date: _____ Location: _____

Prompt or prompt translation:

JOURNAL

Prompt or prompt translation:

....

....

....

....

....

....

....

....

....

....

....

....

....

....

....

....

....

....

....

....

....

....

....

....

....

JOURNAL

Prompt #: ___ Date: ________________ Location: ________________________

Prompt or prompt translation:

JOURNAL

Souvenirs from my journey

You've made it to the end of your language journal and journey! It's time to write down your takeaways from your hard work, dedication, and consistency.

Rate how you feel about your current skill levels from 1 to 7 in the following areas. How has your learning changed?

In what ways has your life or outlook on the world changed from your fluent*ish* experience?

....

....

....

....

....

....

....

....

....

....

....

....

....

....

....

....

What have you learned about yourself? Did something surprise you? Did something become more certain?

....
....
....
....
....
....
....
....

What was your favorite prompt entry? Why?

....
....
....
....
....
....
....
....

What new resources have become a part of your daily life? Think: music, movies, creators, etc.

....
....
....
....
....
....
....
....
....
....
....
....
....
....
....

Write a list of 10 things you want to remember from your fluent*ish* journey.

....
....
....
....
....
....
....
....

Bonus prompt: Share your answers on social media and tag @joclub_ and @TYOpenRoad so we can celebrate your win with you and share your progress with other global minds.

Additional resources

For inspirational sample pages of this journal and other language resources, go to:

www.teachyourself.com
@TYOpenRoad

For additional prompts and journaling ideas, please visit:

www.joclub.world/fluent
 @joclub_

Rely on Teach Yourself®, trusted by language learners for over 85 years.

No matter where you are on your language learning journey or how far you plan to go, **Teach Yourself®** has a course to take you from beginner to confident speaker in over 70 languages.

Written by experienced language teachers, our courses provide an easy-to-follow roadmap to guide your learning and keep you on track. Our bestselling series cover all the skills you need and can be combined with each other, or any other materials, to create a custom learning path to achieve your specific goals.

Whether it's perfecting grammar with one of our Tutors, learning a foreign alphabet with *Script Hacking* or building your vocabulary and reading skills with our delightful *Short Stories* series, **Teach Yourself®** will keep you motivated and moving forward.

Open yourself to endless possibilities. *Love. Work. Travel. Friendship. Brain training. Cultural curiosity.* The road is yours.

@TYOpenRoad

Teach®
Yourself